PRACTICE PLANNER

Juanita Robinson

BrainSwell Publishing
Ingersoll, Ontario

Copyright © 2019 Juanita Robinson

All rights reserved. The use of any part of this publication reproduced, transmitted in any form or by any means, electronic, mechanical, photocopying, recording, or otherwise, or stored in a retrieval system, without the prior written consent of the publisher is an infringement of the copyright law.

ISBN 978-1-989296-14-1

Cover Design copyright © Juanita Robinson

BrainSwell Publishing
Ingersoll, ON

A Note to Singers & Voice Teachers
~Make More of the Time Between Lessons~

Have you ever sat down to practice and wondered what you were supposed to actually work on?

The J.R. Vocal Coaching Practice Planner is a way for singers and voice teachers to communicate expectations in a simple, organized, and effective manner.
It's no secret that in order to improve as a vocalist, a singer has to practice. As a voice teacher, I have found that if students can easily see what they're supposed to practice (even knowing where the exercise starts and ends on the piano), they feel more confident that they can replicate the exercises when they go home to practice. This is why I have included an image of a full piano keyboard under each exercise. Even students without the ability to play the piano can start to understand how to visually interpret the exercise patterns they see on the keyboard.

Although this Practice Planner seems basic, its simplicity is its strength. The planner allows for your teacher to clearly lay out their expectations, and all you have to do is work through the assigned exercises each week. It's like having your teacher beside you each time you practice!

If this practice planner seems too simple for what you feel is needed, you may want to consider the J.R. Vocal Coaching's Practice Journal for Vocalists. The Practice Journal is for more advanced students to record details about their practice habits. In doing so, vocalists can develop and establish healthy patterns in their practice regime.

The J.R. Vocal Coaching Practice Journal for Vocalists can be found on Amazon and most other online bookstores.

Notes:

Short & Long-Term Goals

- _____
- _____
- _____
- _____
- _____
- _____
- _____
- _____
- _____
- _____
- _____
- _____
- _____
- _____
- _____
- _____

Notes:

Repertoire

Songs I'd like to work on	Songs I've mastered	Key

Repertoire

Songs I'd like to work on	Songs I've mastered	Key

Repertoire

Songs I'd like to work on	Songs I've mastered	Key

Weekly Practice Exercises

| 1. | Exercise | Pattern | Register | Purpose |

| 2. | Exercise | Pattern | Register | Purpose |

| 3. | Exercise | Pattern | Register | Purpose |

| 4. | Exercise | Pattern | Register | Purpose |

| 5. | Exercise | Pattern | Register | Purpose |

| 6. | Exercise | Pattern | Register | Purpose |

Song I'm Working On

Notes From My Voice Lesson

Practice Time This Week

Day 1	Day 2	Day 3	Day 4	Day 5
_____ min.	_____ min.	_____ min.	_____ min.	_____ min.

Personal Practice Notes & Observations

Weekly Practice Exercises

| 1. | Exercise | Pattern | Register | Purpose |

| 2. | Exercise | Pattern | Register | Purpose |

| 3. | Exercise | Pattern | Register | Purpose |

| 4. | Exercise | Pattern | Register | Purpose |

| 5. | Exercise | Pattern | Register | Purpose |

| 6. | Exercise | Pattern | Register | Purpose |

Song I'm Working On

Notes From My Voice Lesson

Practice Time This Week

Day 1	Day 2	Day 3	Day 4	Day 5
_____ min.	_____ min.	_____ min.	_____ min.	_____ min.

Personal Practice Notes & Observations

Weekly Practice Exercises

| 1. | Exercise | Pattern | Register | Purpose |

| 2. | Exercise | Pattern | Register | Purpose |

| 3. | Exercise | Pattern | Register | Purpose |

| 4. | Exercise | Pattern | Register | Purpose |

| 5. | Exercise | Pattern | Register | Purpose |

| 6. | Exercise | Pattern | Register | Purpose |

Song I'm Working On

Notes From My Voice Lesson

Practice Time This Week

Day 1	Day 2	Day 3	Day 4	Day 5
_____ min.	_____ min.	_____ min.	_____ min.	_____ min.

Personal Practice Notes & Observations

Weekly Practice Exercises

| 1. | Exercise | Pattern | Register | Purpose |

| 2. | Exercise | Pattern | Register | Purpose |

| 3. | Exercise | Pattern | Register | Purpose |

| 4. | Exercise | Pattern | Register | Purpose |

| 5. | Exercise | Pattern | Register | Purpose |

| 6. | Exercise | Pattern | Register | Purpose |

Song I'm Working On

Notes From My Voice Lesson

Practice Time This Week

Day 1	Day 2	Day 3	Day 4	Day 5
_____ min.	_____ min.	_____ min.	_____ min.	_____ min.

Personal Practice Notes & Observations

Weekly Practice Exercises

| 1. | Exercise | Pattern | Register | Purpose |

| 2. | Exercise | Pattern | Register | Purpose |

| 3. | Exercise | Pattern | Register | Purpose |

| 4. | Exercise | Pattern | Register | Purpose |

| 5. | Exercise | Pattern | Register | Purpose |

| 6. | Exercise | Pattern | Register | Purpose |

Song I'm Working On

Notes From My Voice Lesson

Practice Time This Week

Day 1	Day 2	Day 3	Day 4	Day 5
_____ min.	_____ min.	_____ min.	_____ min.	_____ min.

Personal Practice Notes & Observations

Weekly Practice Exercises

| 1. | Exercise | Pattern | Register | Purpose |

| 2. | Exercise | Pattern | Register | Purpose |

| 3. | Exercise | Pattern | Register | Purpose |

| 4. | Exercise | Pattern | Register | Purpose |

| 5. | Exercise | Pattern | Register | Purpose |

| 6. | Exercise | Pattern | Register | Purpose |

Song I'm Working On

Notes From My Voice Lesson

Practice Time This Week

Day 1	Day 2	Day 3	Day 4	Day 5
_____ min.	_____ min.	_____ min.	_____ min.	_____ min.

Personal Practice Notes & Observations

Weekly Practice Exercises

| 1. | Exercise | Pattern | Register | Purpose |

| 2. | Exercise | Pattern | Register | Purpose |

| 3. | Exercise | Pattern | Register | Purpose |

| 4. | Exercise | Pattern | Register | Purpose |

| 5. | Exercise | Pattern | Register | Purpose |

| 6. | Exercise | Pattern | Register | Purpose |

Song I'm Working On

Notes From My Voice Lesson

Practice Time This Week

Day 1	Day 2	Day 3	Day 4	Day 5
_____ min.	_____ min.	_____ min.	_____ min.	_____ min.

Personal Practice Notes & Observations

Weekly Practice Exercises

| 1. | Exercise | Pattern | Register | Purpose |

| 2. | Exercise | Pattern | Register | Purpose |

| 3. | Exercise | Pattern | Register | Purpose |

| 4. | Exercise | Pattern | Register | Purpose |

| 5. | Exercise | Pattern | Register | Purpose |

| 6. | Exercise | Pattern | Register | Purpose |

Song I'm Working On

Notes From My Voice Lesson

Practice Time This Week

Day 1	Day 2	Day 3	Day 4	Day 5
_____ min.	_____ min.	_____ min.	_____ min.	_____ min.

Personal Practice Notes & Observations

Weekly Practice Exercises

| 1. | Exercise | Pattern | Register | Purpose |

| 2. | Exercise | Pattern | Register | Purpose |

| 3. | Exercise | Pattern | Register | Purpose |

| 4. | Exercise | Pattern | Register | Purpose |

| 5. | Exercise | Pattern | Register | Purpose |

| 6. | Exercise | Pattern | Register | Purpose |

Song I'm Working On

Notes From My Voice Lesson

Practice Time This Week

Day 1	Day 2	Day 3	Day 4	Day 5
_____ min.	_____ min.	_____ min.	_____ min.	_____ min.

Personal Practice Notes & Observations

Weekly Practice Exercises

1.	Exercise	Pattern	Register	Purpose

2.	Exercise	Pattern	Register	Purpose

3.	Exercise	Pattern	Register	Purpose

4.	Exercise	Pattern	Register	Purpose

5.	Exercise	Pattern	Register	Purpose

6.	Exercise	Pattern	Register	Purpose

Song I'm Working On

Notes From My Voice Lesson

Practice Time This Week

Day 1	Day 2	Day 3	Day 4	Day 5
_____ min.	_____ min.	_____ min.	_____ min.	_____ min.

Personal Practice Notes & Observations

Weekly Practice Exercises

| 1. | Exercise | Pattern | Register | Purpose |

| 2. | Exercise | Pattern | Register | Purpose |

| 3. | Exercise | Pattern | Register | Purpose |

| 4. | Exercise | Pattern | Register | Purpose |

| 5. | Exercise | Pattern | Register | Purpose |

| 6. | Exercise | Pattern | Register | Purpose |

Song I'm Working On

Notes From My Voice Lesson

Practice Time This Week

Day 1	Day 2	Day 3	Day 4	Day 5
_____ min.	_____ min.	_____ min.	_____ min.	_____ min.

Personal Practice Notes & Observations

Weekly Practice Exercises

| 1. | Exercise | Pattern | Register | Purpose |

| 2. | Exercise | Pattern | Register | Purpose |

| 3. | Exercise | Pattern | Register | Purpose |

| 4. | Exercise | Pattern | Register | Purpose |

| 5. | Exercise | Pattern | Register | Purpose |

| 6. | Exercise | Pattern | Register | Purpose |

Song I'm Working On

Notes From My Voice Lesson

Practice Time This Week

Day 1	Day 2	Day 3	Day 4	Day 5
_____ min.	_____ min.	_____ min.	_____ min.	_____ min.

Personal Practice Notes & Observations

Weekly Practice Exercises

| 1. Exercise | Pattern | Register | Purpose |

| 2. Exercise | Pattern | Register | Purpose |

| 3. Exercise | Pattern | Register | Purpose |

| 4. Exercise | Pattern | Register | Purpose |

| 5. Exercise | Pattern | Register | Purpose |

| 6. Exercise | Pattern | Register | Purpose |

Song I'm Working On

Notes From My Voice Lesson

Practice Time This Week

Day 1	Day 2	Day 3	Day 4	Day 5
_____ min.	_____ min.	_____ min.	_____ min.	_____ min.

Personal Practice Notes & Observations

Weekly Practice Exercises

| 1. | Exercise | Pattern | Register | Purpose |

| 2. | Exercise | Pattern | Register | Purpose |

| 3. | Exercise | Pattern | Register | Purpose |

| 4. | Exercise | Pattern | Register | Purpose |

| 5. | Exercise | Pattern | Register | Purpose |

| 6. | Exercise | Pattern | Register | Purpose |

Song I'm Working On

Notes From My Voice Lesson

Practice Time This Week

Day 1	Day 2	Day 3	Day 4	Day 5
_____ min.	_____ min.	_____ min.	_____ min.	_____ min.

Personal Practice Notes & Observations

Weekly Practice Exercises

| 1. | Exercise | Pattern | Register | Purpose |

| 2. | Exercise | Pattern | Register | Purpose |

| 3. | Exercise | Pattern | Register | Purpose |

| 4. | Exercise | Pattern | Register | Purpose |

| 5. | Exercise | Pattern | Register | Purpose |

| 6. | Exercise | Pattern | Register | Purpose |

Song I'm Working On

Notes From My Voice Lesson

Practice Time This Week

Day 1	Day 2	Day 3	Day 4	Day 5
_____ min.	_____ min.	_____ min.	_____ min.	_____ min.

Personal Practice Notes & Observations

Weekly Practice Exercises

| 1. | Exercise | Pattern | Register | Purpose |

| 2. | Exercise | Pattern | Register | Purpose |

| 3. | Exercise | Pattern | Register | Purpose |

| 4. | Exercise | Pattern | Register | Purpose |

| 5. | Exercise | Pattern | Register | Purpose |

| 6. | Exercise | Pattern | Register | Purpose |

Song I'm Working On

Notes From My Voice Lesson

Practice Time This Week

Day 1	Day 2	Day 3	Day 4	Day 5
_____ min.	_____ min.	_____ min.	_____ min.	_____ min.

Personal Practice Notes & Observations

Weekly Practice Exercises

| 1. | Exercise | Pattern | Register | Purpose |

| 2. | Exercise | Pattern | Register | Purpose |

| 3. | Exercise | Pattern | Register | Purpose |

| 4. | Exercise | Pattern | Register | Purpose |

| 5. | Exercise | Pattern | Register | Purpose |

| 6. | Exercise | Pattern | Register | Purpose |

Song I'm Working On

Notes From My Voice Lesson

Practice Time This Week

Day 1	Day 2	Day 3	Day 4	Day 5
_____ min.	_____ min.	_____ min.	_____ min.	_____ min.

Personal Practice Notes & Observations

Weekly Practice Exercises

1.	Exercise	Pattern	Register	Purpose

2.	Exercise	Pattern	Register	Purpose

3.	Exercise	Pattern	Register	Purpose

4.	Exercise	Pattern	Register	Purpose

5.	Exercise	Pattern	Register	Purpose

6.	Exercise	Pattern	Register	Purpose

Song I'm Working On

Notes From My Voice Lesson

Practice Time This Week

Day 1	Day 2	Day 3	Day 4	Day 5
_____ min.	_____ min.	_____ min.	_____ min.	_____ min.

Personal Practice Notes & Observations

Weekly Practice Exercises

1.	Exercise	Pattern	Register	Purpose

2.	Exercise	Pattern	Register	Purpose

3.	Exercise	Pattern	Register	Purpose

4.	Exercise	Pattern	Register	Purpose

5.	Exercise	Pattern	Register	Purpose

6.	Exercise	Pattern	Register	Purpose

Song I'm Working On

Notes From My Voice Lesson

Practice Time This Week

Day 1	Day 2	Day 3	Day 4	Day 5
_____ min.	_____ min.	_____ min.	_____ min.	_____ min.

Personal Practice Notes & Observations

Weekly Practice Exercises

1.	Exercise	Pattern	Register	Purpose

2.	Exercise	Pattern	Register	Purpose

3.	Exercise	Pattern	Register	Purpose

4.	Exercise	Pattern	Register	Purpose

5.	Exercise	Pattern	Register	Purpose

6.	Exercise	Pattern	Register	Purpose

Song I'm Working On

Notes From My Voice Lesson

Practice Time This Week

Day 1	Day 2	Day 3	Day 4	Day 5
_____ min.	_____ min.	_____ min.	_____ min.	_____ min.

Personal Practice Notes & Observations

Weekly Practice Exercises

| 1. Exercise | Pattern | Register | Purpose |

| 2. Exercise | Pattern | Register | Purpose |

| 3. Exercise | Pattern | Register | Purpose |

| 4. Exercise | Pattern | Register | Purpose |

| 5. Exercise | Pattern | Register | Purpose |

| 6. Exercise | Pattern | Register | Purpose |

Song I'm Working On

Notes From My Voice Lesson

Practice Time This Week

Day 1	Day 2	Day 3	Day 4	Day 5
_____ min.	_____ min.	_____ min.	_____ min.	_____ min.

Personal Practice Notes & Observations

Weekly Practice Exercises

1.	Exercise	Pattern	Register	Purpose

2.	Exercise	Pattern	Register	Purpose

3.	Exercise	Pattern	Register	Purpose

4.	Exercise	Pattern	Register	Purpose

5.	Exercise	Pattern	Register	Purpose

6.	Exercise	Pattern	Register	Purpose

Song I'm Working On

Notes From My Voice Lesson

Practice Time This Week

Day 1	Day 2	Day 3	Day 4	Day 5
_____ min.	_____ min.	_____ min.	_____ min.	_____ min.

Personal Practice Notes & Observations

Weekly Practice Exercises

| 1. Exercise | Pattern | Register | Purpose |

| 2. Exercise | Pattern | Register | Purpose |

| 3. Exercise | Pattern | Register | Purpose |

| 4. Exercise | Pattern | Register | Purpose |

| 5. Exercise | Pattern | Register | Purpose |

| 6. Exercise | Pattern | Register | Purpose |

Song I'm Working On

Notes From My Voice Lesson

Practice Time This Week

Day 1	Day 2	Day 3	Day 4	Day 5
_____ min.	_____ min.	_____ min.	_____ min.	_____ min.

Personal Practice Notes & Observations

Weekly Practice Exercises

| 1. | Exercise | Pattern | Register | Purpose |

| 2. | Exercise | Pattern | Register | Purpose |

| 3. | Exercise | Pattern | Register | Purpose |

| 4. | Exercise | Pattern | Register | Purpose |

| 5. | Exercise | Pattern | Register | Purpose |

| 6. | Exercise | Pattern | Register | Purpose |

Song I'm Working On

Notes From My Voice Lesson

Practice Time This Week

Day 1	Day 2	Day 3	Day 4	Day 5
_____ min.	_____ min.	_____ min.	_____ min.	_____ min.

Personal Practice Notes & Observations

Weekly Practice Exercises

| 1. | Exercise | Pattern | Register | Purpose |

| 2. | Exercise | Pattern | Register | Purpose |

| 3. | Exercise | Pattern | Register | Purpose |

| 4. | Exercise | Pattern | Register | Purpose |

| 5. | Exercise | Pattern | Register | Purpose |

| 6. | Exercise | Pattern | Register | Purpose |

Song I'm Working On

Notes From My Voice Lesson

Practice Time This Week

Day 1	Day 2	Day 3	Day 4	Day 5
_____ min.	_____ min.	_____ min.	_____ min.	_____ min.

Personal Practice Notes & Observations

Weekly Practice Exercises

1.	Exercise	Pattern	Register	Purpose

2.	Exercise	Pattern	Register	Purpose

3.	Exercise	Pattern	Register	Purpose

4.	Exercise	Pattern	Register	Purpose

5.	Exercise	Pattern	Register	Purpose

6.	Exercise	Pattern	Register	Purpose

Song I'm Working On

Notes From My Voice Lesson

Practice Time This Week

Day 1	Day 2	Day 3	Day 4	Day 5
_____ min.	_____ min.	_____ min.	_____ min.	_____ min.

Personal Practice Notes & Observations

Weekly Practice Exercises

| 1. | Exercise | Pattern | Register | Purpose |

| 2. | Exercise | Pattern | Register | Purpose |

| 3. | Exercise | Pattern | Register | Purpose |

| 4. | Exercise | Pattern | Register | Purpose |

| 5. | Exercise | Pattern | Register | Purpose |

| 6. | Exercise | Pattern | Register | Purpose |

Song I'm Working On

Notes From My Voice Lesson

Practice Time This Week

Day 1	Day 2	Day 3	Day 4	Day 5
_____ min.	_____ min.	_____ min.	_____ min.	_____ min.

Personal Practice Notes & Observations

Weekly Practice Exercises

1.	Exercise	Pattern	Register	Purpose

2.	Exercise	Pattern	Register	Purpose

3.	Exercise	Pattern	Register	Purpose

4.	Exercise	Pattern	Register	Purpose

5.	Exercise	Pattern	Register	Purpose

6.	Exercise	Pattern	Register	Purpose

Song I'm Working On

Notes From My Voice Lesson

Practice Time This Week

Day 1	Day 2	Day 3	Day 4	Day 5
_____ min.	_____ min.	_____ min.	_____ min.	_____ min.

Personal Practice Notes & Observations

Weekly Practice Exercises

| 1. | Exercise | Pattern | Register | Purpose |

| 2. | Exercise | Pattern | Register | Purpose |

| 3. | Exercise | Pattern | Register | Purpose |

| 4. | Exercise | Pattern | Register | Purpose |

| 5. | Exercise | Pattern | Register | Purpose |

| 6. | Exercise | Pattern | Register | Purpose |

Song I'm Working On

Notes From My Voice Lesson

Practice Time This Week

Day 1	Day 2	Day 3	Day 4	Day 5
_____ min.	_____ min.	_____ min.	_____ min.	_____ min.

Personal Practice Notes & Observations

Weekly Practice Exercises

| 1. | Exercise | Pattern | Register | Purpose |

| 2. | Exercise | Pattern | Register | Purpose |

| 3. | Exercise | Pattern | Register | Purpose |

| 4. | Exercise | Pattern | Register | Purpose |

| 5. | Exercise | Pattern | Register | Purpose |

| 6. | Exercise | Pattern | Register | Purpose |

Song I'm Working On

Notes From My Voice Lesson

Practice Time This Week

Day 1	Day 2	Day 3	Day 4	Day 5
_____ min.	_____ min.	_____ min.	_____ min.	_____ min.

Personal Practice Notes & Observations

Weekly Practice Exercises

1. Exercise   Pattern   Register   Purpose

2. Exercise   Pattern   Register   Purpose

3. Exercise   Pattern   Register   Purpose

4. Exercise   Pattern   Register   Purpose

5. Exercise   Pattern   Register   Purpose

6. Exercise   Pattern   Register   Purpose

Song I'm Working On

Notes From My Voice Lesson

Practice Time This Week

Day 1	Day 2	Day 3	Day 4	Day 5
_____ min.	_____ min.	_____ min.	_____ min.	_____ min.

Personal Practice Notes & Observations

Weekly Practice Exercises

| 1. | Exercise | Pattern | Register | Purpose |

| 2. | Exercise | Pattern | Register | Purpose |

| 3. | Exercise | Pattern | Register | Purpose |

| 4. | Exercise | Pattern | Register | Purpose |

| 5. | Exercise | Pattern | Register | Purpose |

| 6. | Exercise | Pattern | Register | Purpose |

Song I'm Working On

Notes From My Voice Lesson

Practice Time This Week

Day 1	Day 2	Day 3	Day 4	Day 5
_____ min.	_____ min.	_____ min.	_____ min.	_____ min.

Personal Practice Notes & Observations

Weekly Practice Exercises

| 1. | Exercise | Pattern | Register | Purpose |

| 2. | Exercise | Pattern | Register | Purpose |

| 3. | Exercise | Pattern | Register | Purpose |

| 4. | Exercise | Pattern | Register | Purpose |

| 5. | Exercise | Pattern | Register | Purpose |

| 6. | Exercise | Pattern | Register | Purpose |

Song I'm Working On

Notes From My Voice Lesson

Practice Time This Week

Day 1	Day 2	Day 3	Day 4	Day 5
_____ min.	_____ min.	_____ min.	_____ min.	_____ min.

Personal Practice Notes & Observations

Weekly Practice Exercises

1.	Exercise	Pattern	Register	Purpose

2.	Exercise	Pattern	Register	Purpose

3.	Exercise	Pattern	Register	Purpose

4.	Exercise	Pattern	Register	Purpose

5.	Exercise	Pattern	Register	Purpose

6.	Exercise	Pattern	Register	Purpose

Song I'm Working On

Notes From My Voice Lesson

Practice Time This Week

Day 1	Day 2	Day 3	Day 4	Day 5
_____ min.	_____ min.	_____ min.	_____ min.	_____ min.

Personal Practice Notes & Observations

Weekly Practice Exercises

| 1. Exercise | Pattern | Register | Purpose |

| 2. Exercise | Pattern | Register | Purpose |

| 3. Exercise | Pattern | Register | Purpose |

| 4. Exercise | Pattern | Register | Purpose |

| 5. Exercise | Pattern | Register | Purpose |

| 6. Exercise | Pattern | Register | Purpose |

Song I'm Working On

Notes From My Voice Lesson

Practice Time This Week

Day 1	Day 2	Day 3	Day 4	Day 5
_____ min.	_____ min.	_____ min.	_____ min.	_____ min.

Personal Practice Notes & Observations

Weekly Practice Exercises

1.	Exercise	Pattern	Register	Purpose

2.	Exercise	Pattern	Register	Purpose

3.	Exercise	Pattern	Register	Purpose

4.	Exercise	Pattern	Register	Purpose

5.	Exercise	Pattern	Register	Purpose

6.	Exercise	Pattern	Register	Purpose

Song I'm Working On

Notes From My Voice Lesson

Practice Time This Week

Day 1	Day 2	Day 3	Day 4	Day 5
_____ min.	_____ min.	_____ min.	_____ min.	_____ min.

Personal Practice Notes & Observations

Weekly Practice Exercises

1. Exercise Pattern Register Purpose

2. Exercise Pattern Register Purpose

3. Exercise Pattern Register Purpose

4. Exercise Pattern Register Purpose

5. Exercise Pattern Register Purpose

6. Exercise Pattern Register Purpose

Song I'm Working On

Notes From My Voice Lesson

Practice Time This Week

Day 1	Day 2	Day 3	Day 4	Day 5
_____ min.	_____ min.	_____ min.	_____ min.	_____ min.

Personal Practice Notes & Observations

Weekly Practice Exercises

| 1. Exercise | Pattern | Register | Purpose |

| 2. Exercise | Pattern | Register | Purpose |

| 3. Exercise | Pattern | Register | Purpose |

| 4. Exercise | Pattern | Register | Purpose |

| 5. Exercise | Pattern | Register | Purpose |

| 6. Exercise | Pattern | Register | Purpose |

Song I'm Working On

Notes From My Voice Lesson

Practice Time This Week

Day 1	Day 2	Day 3	Day 4	Day 5
_____ min.	_____ min.	_____ min.	_____ min.	_____ min.

Personal Practice Notes & Observations

Weekly Practice Exercises

1. Exercise   Pattern   Register   Purpose

2. Exercise   Pattern   Register   Purpose

3. Exercise   Pattern   Register   Purpose

4. Exercise   Pattern   Register   Purpose

5. Exercise   Pattern   Register   Purpose

6. Exercise   Pattern   Register   Purpose

Song I'm Working On

Notes From My Voice Lesson

Practice Time This Week

Day 1	Day 2	Day 3	Day 4	Day 5
_____ min.	_____ min.	_____ min.	_____ min.	_____ min.

Personal Practice Notes & Observations

Weekly Practice Exercises

1.	Exercise	Pattern	Register	Purpose

2.	Exercise	Pattern	Register	Purpose

3.	Exercise	Pattern	Register	Purpose

4.	Exercise	Pattern	Register	Purpose

5.	Exercise	Pattern	Register	Purpose

6.	Exercise	Pattern	Register	Purpose

Song I'm Working On

Notes From My Voice Lesson

Practice Time This Week

Day 1	Day 2	Day 3	Day 4	Day 5
_____ min.	_____ min.	_____ min.	_____ min.	_____ min.

Personal Practice Notes & Observations

Weekly Practice Exercises

| 1. | Exercise | Pattern | Register | Purpose |

| 2. | Exercise | Pattern | Register | Purpose |

| 3. | Exercise | Pattern | Register | Purpose |

| 4. | Exercise | Pattern | Register | Purpose |

| 5. | Exercise | Pattern | Register | Purpose |

| 6. | Exercise | Pattern | Register | Purpose |

Song I'm Working On

Notes From My Voice Lesson

Practice Time This Week

Day 1	Day 2	Day 3	Day 4	Day 5
_____ min.	_____ min.	_____ min.	_____ min.	_____ min.

Personal Practice Notes & Observations

Weekly Practice Exercises

1.	Exercise	Pattern	Register	Purpose

2.	Exercise	Pattern	Register	Purpose

3.	Exercise	Pattern	Register	Purpose

4.	Exercise	Pattern	Register	Purpose

5.	Exercise	Pattern	Register	Purpose

6.	Exercise	Pattern	Register	Purpose

Song I'm Working On

Notes From My Voice Lesson

Practice Time This Week

Day 1	Day 2	Day 3	Day 4	Day 5
_____ min.	_____ min.	_____ min.	_____ min.	_____ min.

Personal Practice Notes & Observations

Weekly Practice Exercises

1. Exercise	Pattern	Register	Purpose

2. Exercise	Pattern	Register	Purpose

3. Exercise	Pattern	Register	Purpose

4. Exercise	Pattern	Register	Purpose

5. Exercise	Pattern	Register	Purpose

6. Exercise	Pattern	Register	Purpose

Song I'm Working On

Notes From My Voice Lesson

Practice Time This Week

Day 1	Day 2	Day 3	Day 4	Day 5
_____ min.	_____ min.	_____ min.	_____ min.	_____ min.

Personal Practice Notes & Observations

Weekly Practice Exercises

| 1. | Exercise | Pattern | Register | Purpose |

| 2. | Exercise | Pattern | Register | Purpose |

| 3. | Exercise | Pattern | Register | Purpose |

| 4. | Exercise | Pattern | Register | Purpose |

| 5. | Exercise | Pattern | Register | Purpose |

| 6. | Exercise | Pattern | Register | Purpose |

Song I'm Working On

Notes From My Voice Lesson

Practice Time This Week

Day 1	Day 2	Day 3	Day 4	Day 5
_____ min.	_____ min.	_____ min.	_____ min.	_____ min.

Personal Practice Notes & Observations

Weekly Practice Exercises

1.	Exercise	Pattern	Register	Purpose

2.	Exercise	Pattern	Register	Purpose

3.	Exercise	Pattern	Register	Purpose

4.	Exercise	Pattern	Register	Purpose

5.	Exercise	Pattern	Register	Purpose

6.	Exercise	Pattern	Register	Purpose

Song I'm Working On

Notes From My Voice Lesson

Practice Time This Week

Day 1	Day 2	Day 3	Day 4	Day 5
_____ min.	_____ min.	_____ min.	_____ min.	_____ min.

Personal Practice Notes & Observations

Weekly Practice Exercises

| 1. | Exercise | Pattern | Register | Purpose |

| 2. | Exercise | Pattern | Register | Purpose |

| 3. | Exercise | Pattern | Register | Purpose |

| 4. | Exercise | Pattern | Register | Purpose |

| 5. | Exercise | Pattern | Register | Purpose |

| 6. | Exercise | Pattern | Register | Purpose |

Song I'm Working On

Notes From My Voice Lesson

Practice Time This Week

Day 1	Day 2	Day 3	Day 4	Day 5
_____ min.	_____ min.	_____ min.	_____ min.	_____ min.

Personal Practice Notes & Observations

Weekly Practice Exercises

| 1. | Exercise | Pattern | Register | Purpose |

| 2. | Exercise | Pattern | Register | Purpose |

| 3. | Exercise | Pattern | Register | Purpose |

| 4. | Exercise | Pattern | Register | Purpose |

| 5. | Exercise | Pattern | Register | Purpose |

| 6. | Exercise | Pattern | Register | Purpose |

Song I'm Working On

Notes From My Voice Lesson

Practice Time This Week

Day 1	Day 2	Day 3	Day 4	Day 5
_____ min.	_____ min.	_____ min.	_____ min.	_____ min.

Personal Practice Notes & Observations

Weekly Practice Exercises

| 1. | Exercise | Pattern | Register | Purpose |

| 2. | Exercise | Pattern | Register | Purpose |

| 3. | Exercise | Pattern | Register | Purpose |

| 4. | Exercise | Pattern | Register | Purpose |

| 5. | Exercise | Pattern | Register | Purpose |

| 6. | Exercise | Pattern | Register | Purpose |

Song I'm Working On

Notes From My Voice Lesson

Practice Time This Week

Day 1	Day 2	Day 3	Day 4	Day 5
_____ min.	_____ min.	_____ min.	_____ min.	_____ min.

Personal Practice Notes & Observations

Weekly Practice Exercises

| 1. | Exercise | Pattern | Register | Purpose |

| 2. | Exercise | Pattern | Register | Purpose |

| 3. | Exercise | Pattern | Register | Purpose |

| 4. | Exercise | Pattern | Register | Purpose |

| 5. | Exercise | Pattern | Register | Purpose |

| 6. | Exercise | Pattern | Register | Purpose |

Song I'm Working On

Notes From My Voice Lesson

Practice Time This Week

Day 1	Day 2	Day 3	Day 4	Day 5
_____ min.	_____ min.	_____ min.	_____ min.	_____ min.

Personal Practice Notes & Observations

Weekly Practice Exercises

| 1. | Exercise | Pattern | Register | Purpose |

| 2. | Exercise | Pattern | Register | Purpose |

| 3. | Exercise | Pattern | Register | Purpose |

| 4. | Exercise | Pattern | Register | Purpose |

| 5. | Exercise | Pattern | Register | Purpose |

| 6. | Exercise | Pattern | Register | Purpose |

Song I'm Working On

Notes From My Voice Lesson

Practice Time This Week

Day 1	Day 2	Day 3	Day 4	Day 5
_____ min.	_____ min.	_____ min.	_____ min.	_____ min.

Personal Practice Notes & Observations

Weekly Practice Exercises

| 1. | Exercise | Pattern | Register | Purpose |

| 2. | Exercise | Pattern | Register | Purpose |

| 3. | Exercise | Pattern | Register | Purpose |

| 4. | Exercise | Pattern | Register | Purpose |

| 5. | Exercise | Pattern | Register | Purpose |

| 6. | Exercise | Pattern | Register | Purpose |

Song I'm Working On

Notes From My Voice Lesson

Practice Time This Week

Day 1	Day 2	Day 3	Day 4	Day 5
_____ min.	_____ min.	_____ min.	_____ min.	_____ min.

Personal Practice Notes & Observations

Weekly Practice Exercises

| 1. | Exercise | Pattern | Register | Purpose |

| 2. | Exercise | Pattern | Register | Purpose |

| 3. | Exercise | Pattern | Register | Purpose |

| 4. | Exercise | Pattern | Register | Purpose |

| 5. | Exercise | Pattern | Register | Purpose |

| 6. | Exercise | Pattern | Register | Purpose |

Song I'm Working On

Notes From My Voice Lesson

Practice Time This Week

Day 1	Day 2	Day 3	Day 4	Day 5
_____ min.	_____ min.	_____ min.	_____ min.	_____ min.

Personal Practice Notes & Observations

Notes:

Notes:

Notes:

Author Bio

Juanita grew up in Southwestern Ontario and has stubbornly refused to move from that area as she confidently believes it is the most beautiful place on earth to live… except during the winter months. She lives with her husband, two sons and two goldfish who are currently grieving the loss of the third goldfish as it explored the filter and did not find the inside of the filter to be conducive to living.

Juanita and her family live in the beautiful town of Ingersoll where she runs J.R. Vocal Coaching out of her home studio.

Passionate about music
Juanita has always loved music—instrumental and vocal.
However, like many people, she used to believe that she was stuck with the voice she was born with. It wasn't until she had the opportunity to take lessons from a very gifted vocal coach that she realized that through warm-ups and technique exercises, she could strengthen her voice, expand her range, and ultimately sing the way she never dreamed she could!

Passionate about teaching
Juanita eventually realized that as much as she loved singing, she was born to teach. Juanita is energized by teaching and showing students that their vocal roadblocks are actually only hurdles.

Trained by the best
Juanita was trained and mentored by Justin Stoney, owner and founder of New York Vocal Coaching. Through and through, Justin is an inspiring and gifted teacher as well as someone who has worked tirelessly to perfect his craft of singing and teaching. Juanita considers herself truly blessed to have been able to learn under him. Justin Stoney has encouraged her and given her the tools she needs to be the best teacher she can be.

I hope you found this planner helpful. I am always looking to improve the planner, and I am excited about hearing from you to learn not only how this book has helped you, but also to find out how I can make the book fit your needs more effectively. I can be contacted through my website at jrvocals.com or by email at jrvocalcoaching@gmail.com

If you enjoyed the book, please also take the time to leave a quick review where you purchased the book or on Amazon or Goodreads. Reviews can help other students know if this book will be beneficial to them.

All the best to you as you continue to perfect your singing voice!

Books by Juanita Robinson
J.R. Vocal Coaching

Practice Planner

Practice Journal

The J.R. Vocal Coaching Practice Planner is a simple planner to assist vocalists and voice teachers to communicate expectations in an organized and effective manner.
This planner allows for the teacher to clearly lay out each vocal exercise, including an option to map out scales on an image of a piano keyboard. All you, the student, have to do is to work through the assigned exercises each week. It's like having your teacher beside you each time you practice!

The J.R. Vocal Coaching Practice Journal is an advanced journal which lays out all your vocal tools, keeping them organized and in one place. This daily vocal practice log is your chance to look for patterns that lead to success or find out what might be hindering your growth as a vocalist. This practical journal is exactly what you need to help you as you become the vocalist you've always wanted to be!

The Practice Planner for Vocalists & Voice Teachers and the Practice Journal for Vocalists can both be found on Amazon and most other online bookstores.

www.ingramcontent.com/pod-product-compliance
Lightning Source LLC
Chambersburg PA
CBHW081155070526
44583CB00021B/2844